Focus on History

edited by Ray Mitchell and Geoffrey Middleton

At the Time of King Alfred

Jane R Osborn

Longman

Who was Alfred the Great?

Who was Alfred the Great? You may have heard the story of how he burned the cakes and that he fought the Danes. You may even have heard him called 'the father of the navy'. People have told stories about him, made up poems and sung songs about his battles and his wisdom, for over 1,000 years. Here is a statue that was put up to him at the beginning of this century, at Wantage in Berkshire, where he was born.

Alfred actually lived. He was a king in England, ruling over Anglo-Saxons, in the 9th century – in fact he was King of the West Saxons. We know quite a lot about him and his people, partly from manuscripts and histories, partly from objects which belonged to them and which are now in museums.

This coin has a portrait of Alfred. It was minted when he was king, so the coiner must have been trying to show Alfred as he was. Do you think it is like the statue?

The other very beautiful object on the right is known as the 'Alfred jewel'. It has Alfred's name on it and was found near Athelney in Somerset (where he is supposed to have burned the cakes).

There are also books written in King Alfred's time. The most important one is *The Anglo-Saxon Chronicle*, a history written in Old English—the language the Anglo-Saxons spoke. Another is *The Life of King Alfred*, written in Latin by Bishop Asser, who was Bishop of Sherborne in Alfred's time.

We can listen to legends about Alfred and they may or may not be true. We can read what history says about him and what people of his own time said about him. We can look at objects that belong to his time.

These are some of the ways in which we can find out something about Alfred the Great and his people. Perhaps when you have finished this book, you too will want to write the story of his life or a poem about him, or paint pictures of some of the things he did and how people lived in the time when he was alive.

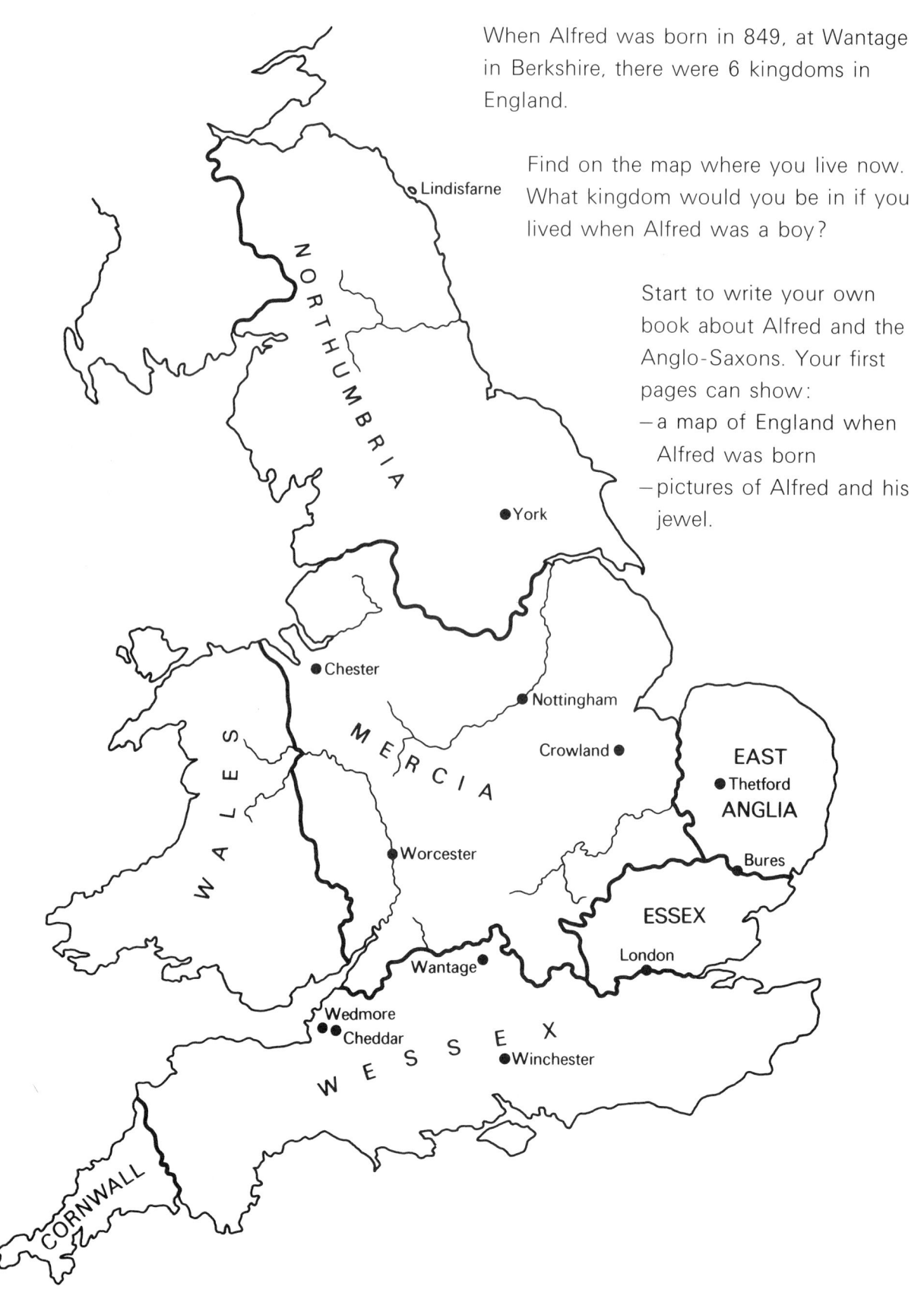

When Alfred was born in 849, at Wantage
in Berkshire, there were 6 kingdoms in
England.

Find on the map where you live now.
What kingdom would you be in if you
lived when Alfred was a boy?

Start to write your own
book about Alfred and the
Anglo-Saxons. Your first
pages can show:
—a map of England when
 Alfred was born
—pictures of Alfred and his
 jewel.

Lindisfarne

NORTHUMBRIA

York

Chester

MERCIA

Nottingham

Crowland

EAST
Thetford
ANGLIA

WALES

Worcester

Bures

ESSEX

Wantage

London

Wedmore
Cheddar

WESSEX

Winchester

CORNWALL

Alfred was the fourth son of King Aethelwulf, who was King of the West Saxons. (That is what the people of Wessex were called. The people of Northumbria were Northumbrians, the people of Mercia were Mercians and the people of East Anglia were East Angles. What do you think the people of Essex were called? If you look at the names Wessex and West Saxons you will probably be able to work it out.)

Above is a silver coin of King Aethelwulf. It has the king's head on it, though the likeness is not very good. Notice the king's name AETHELWULF REX. (The Anglo-Saxon letter Đ means the 'th' sound, and REX means 'king' in Latin.)

Here is a gold ring that probably belonged to King Aethelwulf. Can you see his name spelt out on the band round the bottom?

Besides his 3 brothers, Alfred had a sister, called Aethelswith. She was married to Burgred, King of the Mercians. Here is her ring, also made of gold. Her name was written inside the ring.

In your book add pictures of Aethelwulf's coin and ring, and Aethelswith's ring.

5

Anglo-Saxon halls

Anglo-Saxon kings and their families did not live all the time in one place. Because they needed to know what was going on in the various parts of their kingdom, they had a number of different 'halls', and would travel about from one to another, taking their families and some of their important servants or helpers with them. They would stop for a while at each place, to see the people there, to carry out justice, to find out about the farm affairs, and to see that taxes and fines were being paid properly.

the royal 'palace' at Cheddar

One of the West Saxon royal halls was at Cheddar in Somerset. Its remains have been dug up by archaeologists, so we know a great deal about it. Look carefully at the picture on the opposite page. It shows what Cheddar may have been like when Alfred was a boy and went there with his father.

The big hall in the middle is where the king acted as a judge and met important people. Everyone ate there together, amused themselves there in the evenings, and many of the king's attendants and soldiers — perhaps even his sons — slept there at night. The king himself would sleep in one of the smaller huts round the hall, perhaps in the important-looking one on the left. The queen and her women would also not live in the hall but in the small huts, which were called 'bowers'.

Other huts would be used for various other things. Can you see one which might be a byre for the cattle? And one which might be used for cooking? (Why do you think this?) Corn might also be ground nearby. Can you think of anything else it would be useful to be able to do? Notice the surrounding ditches (for drainage) and the stockade (for safety against wild animals which might attack the cattle). In the woods round about men would hunt for meat.

What else can you find:
— inside the stockade
— outside it?

Make drawings of all the important things in the picture and write a few notes on each for your book.

Make a model of the stockade, the king's hall and the other buildings and things you have found. Paint a large frieze of another Anglo-Saxon village.

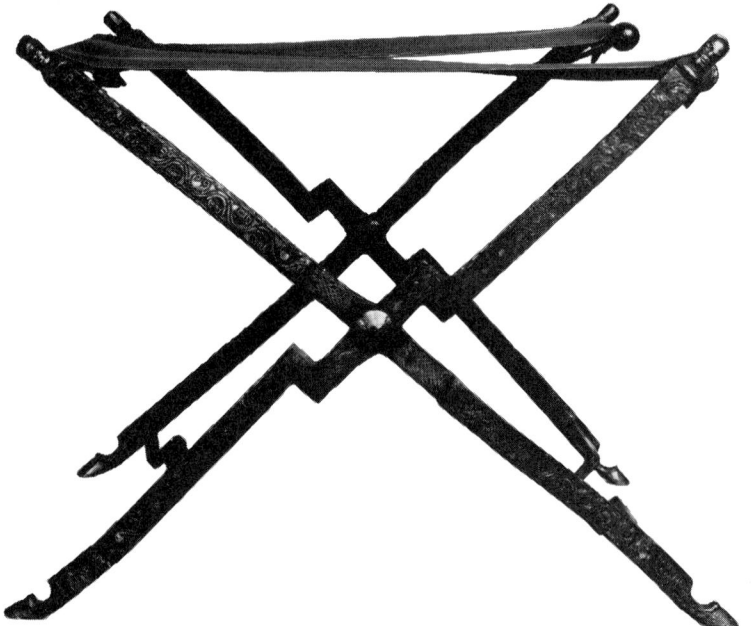

pottery for general household use

Inside the hall everyone would eat their meals, probably off one big table—made of planks put on trestles—with benches to sit on. The king, and perhaps other important people too, would not sit on a bench but on his own stool, like this one, which is now in the British Museum.

Can you see how beautifully decorated the metal legs are, with a head at the top of each one? This piece of furniture must have belonged to someone special. Notice that it could be folded up, to carry on journeys.

On the table there would be wooden platters and pottery of various shapes and sizes, to hold some kinds of food, such as stews, and of course drink.

The king's household would probably also drink out of glass. Not very much Anglo-Saxon glassware has been found (even broken!), so it must have been rare and valuable.

Here is an Anglo-Saxon glass goblet and a glass drinking horn. The glass is quite thick and is a greenish colour. You can see that they are quite highly decorated. These would have been very precious objects, not to have been touched by children!

After the evening meal, people amused themselves in various ways. We know that they played with dice, for instance, and chess.

Here are a knight and a pawn from a chess set made of whalebone which was found at Witchampton in Dorset.

But the way in which the Anglo-Saxons most liked to enjoy themselves was by listening to or playing the harp, or lyre, and singing or saying long poems which told heroic stories about the great deeds of famous men. Remains of musical instruments have been found buried in mounds, sometimes with their dead owners.

Below is a lyre which was put together from wood fragments found in the ship burial at Sutton Hoo. (You can read about this in the *Focus on History* book, *Saxons and Vikings*.)

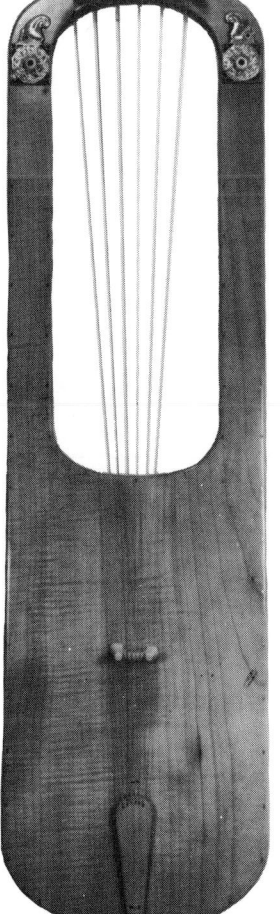

On the right of the lyre is a king (King David in an illustration from a version of the Bible) playing a lyre like this. Notice how he plays it, holding it with his right hand and fingering the strings with his left.

Alfred would certainly have learned to play an instrument. Almost everybody was expected to play and sing if they were asked and only very poor people would not have been able to do so. There is a story about Alfred which tells how he played the harp and sang, in disguise, in a camp full of his enemies.

9

The king's duties

A king in Anglo-Saxon times was called 'the father of his people'. He was, of course, the most important man in his kingdom and people had to do as he said. But in return he had to do a number of tasks which were sometimes quite difficult.

The king was the law-giver. He had to make the laws with the help of his councillors and then he had to travel round from place to place to see that the laws were being obeyed and that justice was being done. In each important place the king would hold a court of justice and anyone could bring his complaints to him. In Anglo-Saxon days there was a fine for every sort of crime. People were not sent to prison — there were no prisons. If a man killed another man, he had to pay a fine called 'wergild' to the relations of the man who had been killed. Do you think this rule was sensible? Why?

A king also had to give gifts to the people who served him. This was a kind of payment, of course, but it was not made in money. He might give a piece of jewellery. He might give a grant of some land, but the land-holder would be bound to do him a certain service in return. Or he might give a fine weapon like this sword which has a strong blade and a gold pommel on its hilt.

Here is another fine sword-pommel, found in London. Look carefully and you will see the many different kinds of pattern. See how many different kinds you can copy. This elaborate piece of work would have been a very suitable gift from a king.

Another task the king had was to lead his people in battle and to make sure that his noblemen and his sons knew how to use their weapons and lead their men.

The weapon they most often used was a sword—like the one on the opposite page. They would also carry long knives, like the two on the left. Both these knives would have had handles, perhaps made of wood or bone or horn, now rotted away. They have writing on them to tell who made them—the smiths must have been proud of their work.

Some noblemen were archers rather than swordsmen. Their bows were made of wood, of course, and we have not found any remains of bows in this country. But we do find arrowheads, like this one.

For protection in battle, the king and his noblemen would wear helmets. Below is what remains of a very grand helmet, which was found at Benty Grange in Derbyshire. The metal bands are iron and the space in between was filled by horn. The animal on the top is a boar—perhaps the man who owned the helmet thought the boar's fierceness would help him.

Also for protection, they would carry shields. Most of the shield would be made of wood and has rotted away. But the central part, called the boss, was usually made of metal and these are sometimes found. The boss below is all that remains of an Anglo-Saxon shield, found at Wretton in Norfolk.

Add a section to your book on Anglo-Saxon weapons and make drawings and write notes about them.

Kings were crowned by bishops in a coronation ceremony in a church — rather as our Queen Elizabeth II was crowned in Westminster Abbey. Here is a picture of King Edmund of the East Angles being crowned at Bures in Suffolk. (It was drawn and painted 300 years later than King Alfred's time.)

It is very likely that Alfred went to meet King Edmund, perhaps at his coronation, perhaps later. It was usual for kings to send their sons to meet other kings, especially on important occasions. They wanted to make sure that the other kings were friendly to them. If you were ruling a kingdom you did not want neighbouring kings to attack you and if you were attacked by someone else you wanted your neighbours to help you.

Anglo-Saxon ladies

Of course there were queens and princesses too—though they were not called 'queen' or 'princess' but 'lady'. Here is a picture of some royal ladies.

Though the picture shows them as saints, they are dressed like ladies of the court and have crowns on their heads. This is one of the best pictures we have of how noble ladies were dressed. Look carefully and you will see the different layers of clothes. There is a long under-tunic, which has sleeves. Over it is a mantle, which seems to have a girdle or belt. On top is the headdress, covering the hair and neck completely.

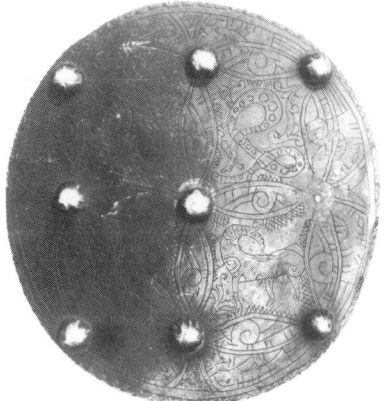

This silver brooch belonged to a woman called Aedwyn. We know this because her name is on the back, cursing any thief who might steal the brooch!

Ladies often wore jewellery. Here is a necklace from Desborough in Northamptonshire, which probably belonged to someone quite important. It is made of garnets and gold—the 'wire' is twisted gold.

Add a section to your book on Anglo-Saxon jewellery. Draw examples and write notes on each piece.

Charlemagne and his empire

Across the Channel there was a very important kingdom indeed — the Empire of the Franks, shown here.

Look in a present-day atlas and find out what we nowadays call the countries or parts of countries that were once in the Frankish Empire.

All this empire was built up and ruled by one man, called Charlemagne (his name means 'Charles the Great'), who was crowned Emperor in 800.

Below is his statue, which shows how he may have looked. Look at the way he is dressed — the ornamental border on his cloak, the big brooch on his shoulder. What is he carrying? If you look at some pictures of the British crown jewels, you will see that our queen carried objects very like these at her coronation. Look back at page 12 and see what King Edmund carried at *his* coronation.

Here is Charlemagne's throne, which can be seen in the cathedral at Aachen, in Germany. It was on this throne that Charlemagne was crowned and from it he ruled his court and his empire.

Charlemagne was a great king. He not only built up his empire, but he ruled it wisely. He made laws and saw that they were carried out and he encouraged learning. He started a palace school for the sons of his noblemen so that they could learn to read and write and he encouraged scholars to come from other countries, including England.

When Charlemagne died, his kingdom had to be split up between his sons and, later, his grandsons. The 3 smaller kingdoms are shown on the map opposite. Can you see which of our present-day countries went into which kingdom? Where is Belgium? Where is Holland?

The empire of the Franks was very rich for a long time. Below is a magnificent piece of church treasure which was made at Charlemagne's court. Look at the many different kinds of jewel. They are set in gold.

Here are two more beautiful objects. The top one is called the talisman of Charlemagne and may have belonged to him. The bottom one, which is made of crystal and engraved with scenes from the Bible, belonged to his great-grandson, Lothar II.

Both these precious things were probably used as pieces of jewellery, perhaps worn round the king's neck. The word 'talisman' means 'luck-piece' and people may have thought that it helped to make and keep Charlemagne a great king.

Farming

We know quite a lot about the way ordinary people lived at the time of the Anglo-Saxons. Their books (which were all written by hand and were called manuscripts) had many pictures in them. For instance, a book of psalms would have a picture of a shepherd and his flock to illustrate the psalm about a shepherd. There were calendars, too, which had pictures to illustrate what went on at each season of the year. The pictures on the next few pages are all taken from Anglo-Saxon manuscripts.

Here are two men with spades, one digging and the other holding up his spade so that it is easy for us to see its shape. Notice that the blade juts out on only one side of the handle and that there is no cross-piece at the top of the handle. Do you think it would have been difficult to use an Anglo-Saxon spade? Why do you think this? Can you see the extra piece at the bottom of the blade that the second man is holding? This is the 'shoe', a piece that was added to strengthen the tool and make it last longer.

Ordinary people had a hard life. This manuscript picture shows a man ploughing the land with oxen. Can you see how they are yoked together (joined by a piece of wood across their shoulders) and how difficult it looks to work the ground?

Another way we know what the Anglo-Saxons did in everyday life is from a book written by Archbishop Aelfric. It is a book of conversations to help boys learn Latin and the conversations are all about day-to-day life. Aelfric's ploughman says:

'I work very hard. I go out at dawn to lead the oxen to the fields. However bitterly cold the winter is I dare not hide at home, but I have to yoke the oxen and fasten them to the plough with its share and coulter. Every day I have to plough an acre or more.'

The share is the iron blade on a plough which cuts the furrow. The coulter is the upright blade in front of the share which cuts up the earth. Find them in the picture.

Aelfric's ploughman had a boy to help him. This boy had to goad the oxen (a goad is a sharp implement mounted on a stick) to make them work and to encourage them by shouting. Look for the ploughman's boy and his goad. He had to help the ploughman feed and water the oxen and clean out their stall. Write a story in your book about being a ploughman's boy.

There was another man who helped look after the oxen. He was the ox-herd. His job was to keep them safe at night and see that wolves did not get to them.

17

Look back at the picture on page 17 and notice the
man walking behind the ploughman. He is sowing the
seed in the ground. When the seed had grown up into
corn and the corn had ripened, it was ready to be
harvested.

Above is a manuscript picture of men reaping the corn
with sickles, gathering it up in sheaves and tossing it
into a cart where another man is stacking
it up with a pitchfork. Men still use the
same kind of tools today in poor parts of
the world and where the land is too steep
or rocky to use machines for the harvest.

Grass was harvested too, for making into hay, just as it is today (except of course that the Anglo-Saxons had no machines to do it). It was harvested with scythes.

We can see Anglo-Saxon scythes in museums. The scythe-blade below, found at Hurbuck in Co. Durham can now be seen in the British Museum.

Below is a manuscript picture of 6 men haymaking—mowing with scythes. Can you see the one sharpening his blade? And the one who is just resting?

When the corn had been harvested, the ears had to be separated from the stalks. This is called 'threshing' and the Anglo-Saxons did it with flails — jointed tools with which they hit, or thrashed, the piles of corn.

Here the corn is being carried into a barn in a big basket. You can see how big the basket is by the way the two men are carrying it slung from a pole. This basket would have been woven from willow twigs by some of the women on the estate. Two other men are threshing the corn with their flails. Notice how long these are and how hard the men seem to be working — the expressions on their faces will tell you that.

The last stage is shown on the right-hand side of the picture. This is winnowing, or sieving, to separate the grain from the outer husk. This has been partly done by the threshing. Then a man sorts it through with his hands while another man fans the husks, or chaff, away.

Now the grain will be stored away, some to be saved for seed to sow next spring, some to make bread through the seasons until harvest comes again. This grain harvest was very important, because it provided the main food-supply. Is it so important nowadays? Why do you think this?

Look carefully at the pictures again to see what clothes the men are wearing and how they are different in winter and summer.

Of course there were other ways in which men got food. They kept herds of cattle, which were used for meat and milk, as well as for ploughing the land. They kept flocks of sheep too.

Above is another picture which illustrates the calendar for May. It shows some shepherds with their sheep. It looks comfortable and peaceful—perhaps it was sunny weather. But Aelfric has a shepherd who does not seem so happy. He says:

'Early in the morning I drive out the sheep to their pastures, and stand over them in heat and cold with my dogs, in case wolves eat them up.

'I lead them into their folds and milk them twice a day, and make butter and cheese from the milk.'

So it was quite hard work and could be dangerous too.

This picture shows another kind of flock—a flock of goats. Here the ground looks stonier than it does in the picture of the shepherds, for goats can find food where sheep cannot.

The life of a goat-herd might have been even harder than a shepherd's. He, too, would milk his goats and make butter and cheese from the milk. He might have to shear his goats for their hair, too, just as the shepherd would shear his sheep for the wool. The women would then spin and weave warm clothes for the winter.

Write a section in your book on 'Anglo-Saxon Farming'. Draw pictures and write notes about: digging, ploughing, sowing, reaping and winnowing corn, and shepherds. Make models and paint friezes about each.

Hunting

Men also found food by hunting for it. Here men are hunting birds, or 'fowling'. Can you tell which is the lord? The other is the fowler. What is the lord carrying in his left hand? He has a hawk on his other wrist which will attack the other birds in the picture. How many can you find and what are they? The large bird, a heron, is probably hunting for fish. Aelfric's fowler says that he catches birds with nets, traps and birdlime as well. (Birdlime is a kind of paste spread on twigs to catch small birds.)

This is another kind of hunting—boar hunting. Look for wild boar in a forest, a hunter with a long spear and another man with two hounds and a horn. Aelfric's huntsman says that the hounds will drive the boar towards the hunter with the spear, who has to stand firm and kill his boar. This was extremely dangerous for the hunter, as wild boar are very fierce and strong.

Men hunted other kinds of animal, such as deer and hares, and of course they also fished. According to Aelfric, they generally thought that fishing in the sea was too dangerous (and this was probably true, because they did not have very good boats). But they fished in rivers and lakes, and caught pike and eel and quite a lot of different kinds of fish that we nowadays would not think very good to eat. Of course there were some fishermen who did fish in the sea and caught the kind of fish that we eat today, such as herrings.

Here is an Anglo-Saxon fish-hook, used by fishermen at Sandtun, near West Hythe in Kent.

Add a section on hunting and fishing to your book. Make a frieze of a boar hunt.

Homes

What kind of houses did the ordinary people live in? Most of the houses have now rotted away because they were mainly built of wood, but the remains of a few have been found.

They might have lived in huts like the small ones in the picture of Anglo-Saxon Cheddar on page 6. That size would have been quite large enough for one family. The walls were made of wattle and daub (interwoven wooden rods plastered with mud and twigs) and the roof was probably thatched. The floor might be paved with stone or it might be made of beaten earth. In the middle of this floor there was a hearth for the fire where the family would cook and warm themselves. Above the hearth was a hole in the roof to let most of the smoke out. But the inside of the hut would still be very smoky when the fire was lighted.

Or, these ordinary people might have lived in a much larger house, as part of a larger 'family' or group.

This is how such a house found at Chalton in Hampshire might have been built. Find the timber walls and thatched roof. If you look carefully at the nearer end, you will see that the open space inside the house has been divided off into smaller spaces. Perhaps these were rooms where separate families could sleep.

Which kind of house would you have liked to live in? Draw a picture of it in your book. Don't forget the smoke coming out of the hole in the roof! Make a model of the house, using parts of branches from trees and straw for the roof.

Not everyone lived and worked on farms or country estates. Some people lived in towns (which were not very large and would probably seem like villages to us) and worked at various trades.

This is how part of the town of Thetford, in Norfolk, probably looked in Anglo-Saxon times. Look at the different kinds of houses. Work out what they were built of and how they were built. The nearest one is rather like the one at Chalton, except that it is larger. Many people could live there and perhaps carry on different kinds of work, too. Then there are some smaller houses—one of them has a paddock by it, perhaps for pasturing animals. There is also a small hut which may have been just a shelter.

Can you make a model of one of these buildings? The model of a Saxon hut on the left, may help you. You will need some short lengths of wood, some dried grass or straw, a hard base and some clay. Label your model and describe how you made your Anglo-Saxon building. Join with your friends to make an Anglo-Saxon town by putting your houses and workplaces together.

Look again at the picture of Thetford. How many people are there in it? They all look very busy. What are they doing? What else can you find in the picture? Make a list of all you find. Then check again in case you have missed anything. Describe how the people are dressed.

25

Crafts and trades

One of the things that the Thetford people are doing in the picture is looking after the pottery kilns. You can see uncovered kilns behind the long house in the picture on page 25. Here is a model of how one of these kilns worked.

The pottery, which of course would be made inside one of the huts, is stacked in layers in the upper part of the kiln and a fire is lighted underneath and around it. Notice the smoke-holes at the top and the man stoking up the fire at the stoke-hole at the bottom.

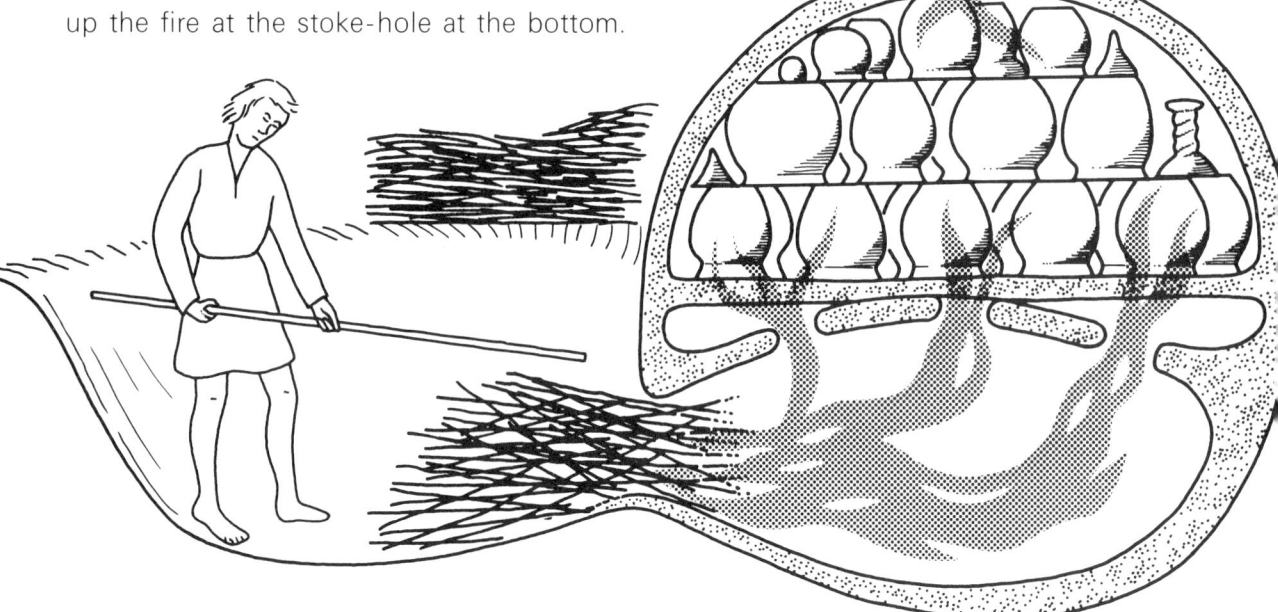

This is a photograph of this same kiln as it was found. It shows the thick outside walls of the kiln, the stoke-hole, the floor for the bottom layer of pots to rest on and the smoke-holes in it. The top part of the kiln had collapsed.

Here are some of the things that the Anglo-Saxon potters of Thetford made. On the right is a kind of lamp. The top would hold oil and a wick.

These bowls were actually found inside the kiln where they were being fired. The kiln had collapsed on top of them.

Archaeologists (people who discover and study ancient things) often have to spend months trying to piece together crumbling pieces. Can you see how this Anglo-Saxon storage jar has been carefully put together again? Look at the thumb marks made by the potter round the rim and down the side to decorate it.

The potters of Thetford made many more jars than they themselves or even all the townspeople would need. They traded them to the country people round about, either for food, or for money to buy food and other things.

On the right is a spouted pitcher which contained a liquid—probably water or ale.

27

Another trade carried on in towns like Thetford was metal working. Aelfric, in his book, writes about various kinds of smith who worked in gold, silver and bronze, as well as in iron. Goldsmiths and silversmiths would work for kings and great men. In Thetford the smiths worked in iron and bronze. Here are some of their tools.

If you look in a metal workshop today, you will see that some of the tools are very like these.

wedge

head of
a hammer

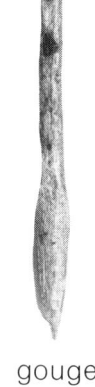

gouge

file

This stone mould was used for casting a bronze, cross-shaped pendant. The little cross beside it is a modern wax casting made from the mould. Can you see how clearly the pattern has come out?

The smiths made all kinds of things needed in everyday Anglo-Saxon life.

All the objects on the opposite page can be found in museums. Try to find some in your local museum.

Add more drawings and notes in your book on:
– Anglo-Saxon pottery and kilns
– Anglo-Saxon metal workers and the things they made.

28

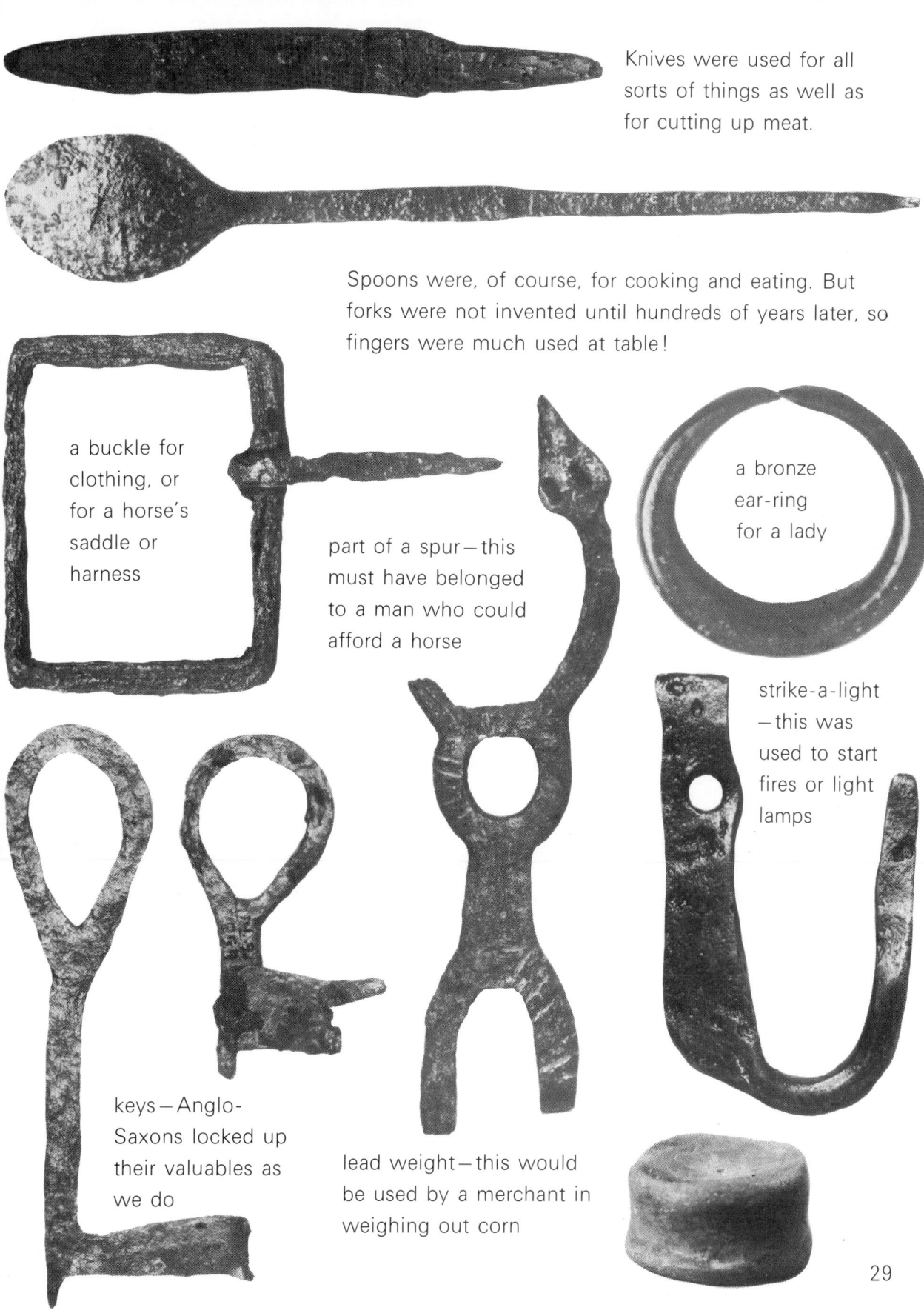

Knives were used for all sorts of things as well as for cutting up meat.

Spoons were, of course, for cooking and eating. But forks were not invented until hundreds of years later, so fingers were much used at table!

a buckle for clothing, or for a horse's saddle or harness

part of a spur—this must have belonged to a man who could afford a horse

a bronze ear-ring for a lady

strike-a-light —this was used to start fires or light lamps

keys—Anglo-Saxons locked up their valuables as we do

lead weight—this would be used by a merchant in weighing out corn

29

Another trade in Thetford was carving things from bone. Some of them were useful things like those shown here.

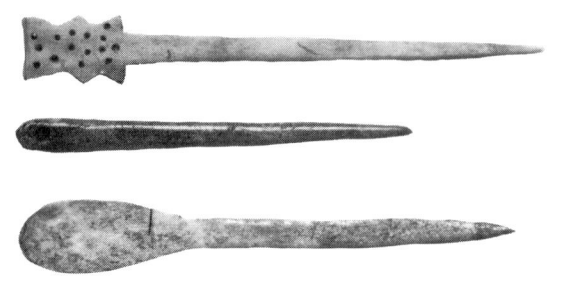

pin and needle — the women sewed with linen thread, wool, or narrow leather thonging

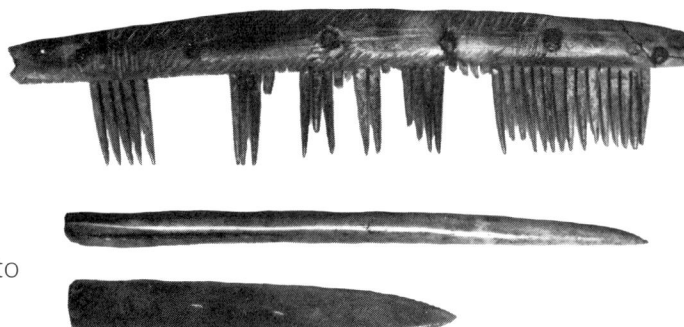

spoon — compare it with the metal one shown on page 29

comb — these are found quite often but they mostly have their teeth broken or missing. Notice the pattern and the way the teeth are put into the double-sided back.

pottery-making tools — these were used to produce a smooth, shining surface

Some of the things were to help people amuse themselves.

flute — this was rather like a 'penny whistle' of today but made from a hollow bone. It would be much easier to play than the harp or lyre (see page 9).

skate — this would be tied on to the shoe or boot with leather thongs. The skater slides along the ice, instead of cutting into it as present-day skaters do.

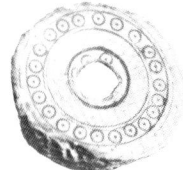

draughtsman — notice the pattern and remember how many more the maker would have had to carve to make up a full set. Look back at the chessmen on page 9 to remind yourself of another game played with pieces made of carved bone or teeth.

The people who bought these things must have had money to spare. Or perhaps the makers made them for themselves. Look for such things in your local museum.

Another trade was spinning and weaving cloth for sale. In most homes the women did weaving—even queens and princesses. But still more cloth was needed for trade, so there were also houses where many women together wove cloth for sale.

Below is some of the equipment that was used by these Anglo-Saxon women and girls for making lengths of cloth. First the wool or flax had to be spun into thread on a spindle held in the hand. The spinning wheel was not invented until hundreds of years later. Then the thread had to be woven.

spindle whorls for spinning
the thread from wool or flax

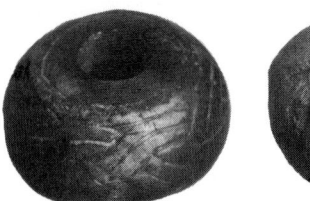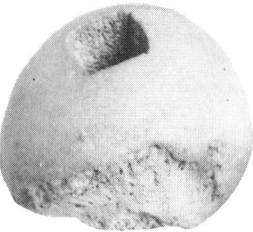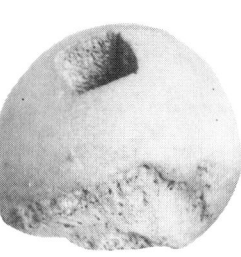

woman spinning on a spindle

one of the weights which were used to keep the loom threads straight

When the piece of cloth was finished it had to be cut from the loom with special iron shears like those below.

Add a chapter on weaving to your book, with your own illustrations and notes.

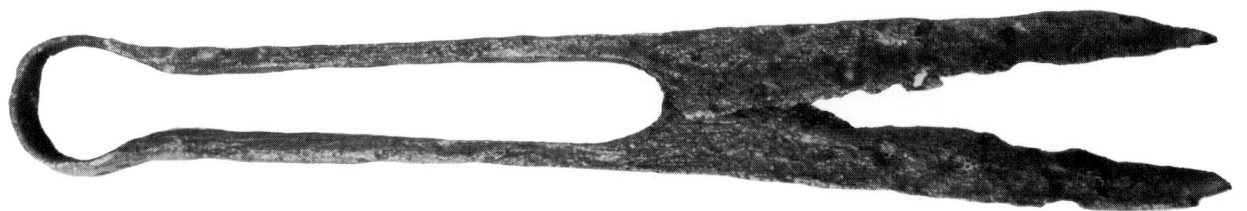

Churches, books and learning

There were many churches in Anglo-Saxon England as it was a Christian land. Most people went to church every day and the work of priests and monks was looked on as being just as valuable as that of soldiers or labourers.

We can still see some Anglo-Saxon churches, or parts of them, today. Many of them were built in wood — most of these have long since been rebuilt. But this church at Greensted, in Essex, still has Saxon timbers built into one of its walls. You can see that these timbers are simply tree-trunks cut down the middle. This is how most early Saxon churches would have looked.

By King Alfred's time most parish churches were built in stone, like this one at Bradford-on-Avon in Wiltshire, which Alfred would have known. They usually had very high walls and steep roofs and look a little bare to modern eyes.

Some of the churches were decorated inside with scenes from the Bible and the lives of the saints painted on the walls. Only a few remains of these paintings can be seen today.

There were also bigger churches known as 'minsters' — cathedrals or monasteries which were looked after by monks. This is the Saxon cathedral at North Elmham, in Norfolk, as it may have looked in Alfred's day. Part of it is built in stone and part in timber framing. The roofs are thatched. How is it like either of the two other smaller churches?

The monks' chief task was of course to pray and to hold the services of the day (and there were 7 of these). But they did other things as well. They looked after the poor, giving them food and medicine, and they were very often the only group of people in the neighbourhood who could read and write. This meant that anyone who wanted his son to learn to do these things would send him to the minster to be taught.

There were no printed books in those times. All books had to be written out by hand, and this was done by monks. They often illustrated them quite beautifully, too.

This is part of a manuscript written out by a monk. It is the beginning of a psalm and the very grand initial letter M shows where the psalm starts. This letter was brightly coloured, or 'illuminated'. The larger letters are the Latin words of the psalm and are neatly and carefully written. The small writing was filled in later and is an Old English translation of the Latin.

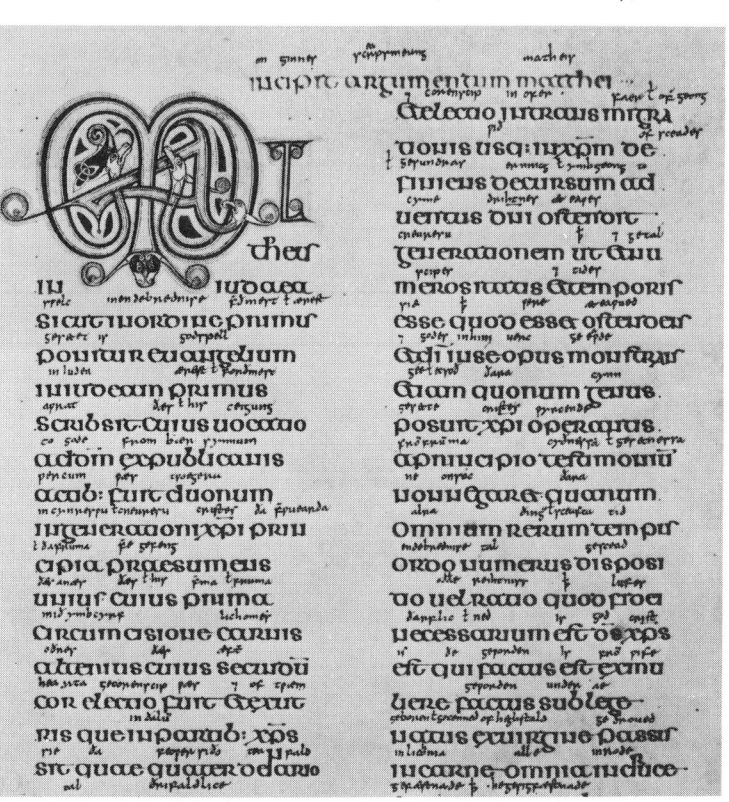

Books were very rare and if a monastery owned one monks would copy it so that people in other places could read it too.

This panel made of ivory (which, in fact, is not English but Frankish) shows monks of this time writing or copying manuscripts. It shows the different ways in which they worked. The largest man, who is probably the most important and may be the writer of the book, has quite a comfortable desk, with a foot-rest and a sloping top. This top even has a ledge, so that the book will not slide off. Look at the bird on the monk's shoulder. It is a dove which is cooing in his ear. This is a way of showing how the monk was inspired by the Holy Spirit.

The men at the bottom are probably copyists and they have no desks, though the one in the middle seems to have a board to lean on. Notice the ink-horn that he is holding in his left hand. The pens might be quills, although they do not look much like it. How are all the monks holding their pens?

Copy the first 6 verses of any psalm you like and illuminate the first letter as the monks did. Remember that if you were a monk your writing would have to be perfect!

From books in the library, find out more about:

—Anglo-Saxon churches and minsters

—monasteries and the lives of monks.

Alfred in Rome

When he was still quite a young boy, Alfred was sent to Rome to see the pope and get a special blessing from him. There were quite a number of English people living in Rome then and Alfred would have stayed with them in the part called the English quarter, where there was a school. In Rome today you can still see some of the things that Alfred would have seen

The arches and pillars of this church—the church of San Clemente—are as they were in Alfred's time. Compare them with the Anglo-Saxon hall and huts in the picture on page 6.

On the walls below the pillars are paintings which were new when Alfred saw them. One shows this crowd of people dressed in the clothes of the 9th century.

Draw a picture of these people in your book and call it 'Romans of Alfred's time'.

Alfred and the Franks

Alfred's father, King Aethelwulf, also went to Rome. People from England usually travelled to Italy through the land of the western Franks. (That country is now part of France. Can you think how France got its name?) As he went home, probably taking Alfred with him, he stopped at the court of the king and married the king's daughter, Judith. So Alfred had a new stepmother, who was the great-granddaughter of Charlemagne.

This is a picture of Judith's father, King Charles, from a psalm book which belonged to him. You can see how rich the court was. The throne is jewelled as well as the crown. How is this picture different from the one of King Edmund on page 12?

Here is a piece of church plate used at Charles's court. How many jewels can you count? They are set in gold. The goldfish are gold, too.

36

The Franks had very beautiful books. This one has gold lettering on purple parchment, with patterns round the border. Can you draw the different designs on this page? You will find that there are at least 3 kinds, as well as the portraits of the 3 apostles.

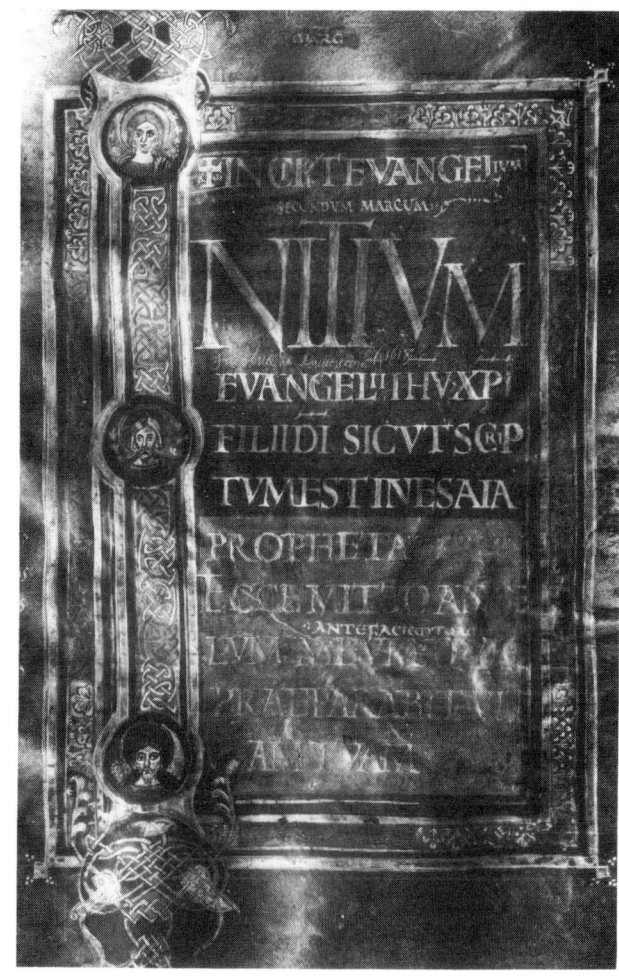

This book cover is made of gold with jewels set into it. Where have you seen anything like these patterns before? Why would you think that books were very valuable things to the Franks?

Draw and colour the cover for your book about Alfred's times. See how many different patterns you can use.

There is a story that, when Alfred was a boy of 12, his mother decided that he and his brothers ought to learn to read. (If the story is true, this must have been his Frankish stepmother, Judith, who came from a court where everyone knew how to read.) The story goes on to say that, although he was the youngest, he was the quickest to learn and so he won the prize—a book of Anglo-Saxon poems.

But why didn't Alfred and his brothers already know how to read? There had been a time, as Alfred himself said later, when there had been so much learning in England that people from other lands had come there to be taught. The greatest scholar at Charlemagne's court had been Alcuin, who came from York. And we have seen that the monasteries produced books and taught boys in their schools.

a page from the Lindisfarne gospels, made by the monks

The most famous centres of learning had been in the north – 'beyond the Humber', as the Anglo-Saxons said. At York, at Jarrow and Monkwearmouth on the Tyne and on the island of Lindisfarne in particular, the monks made beautiful manuscripts, taught in their schools and sent teachers out far and wide. (You can read more about Lindisfarne in the book *Saxons and Vikings* in this *Focus on History* series.)

A very famous scholar, whom we call the Venerable Bede, lived all his life at Monkwearmouth and wrote a great historical book in Latin called *Ecclesiastical History of the English People*. (The word 'ecclesiastical' means that it was to do with the Church, but the book is about other things as well.) Here is part of a page of a copy of the manuscript. It is in Latin, but can you see how clear the writing is?

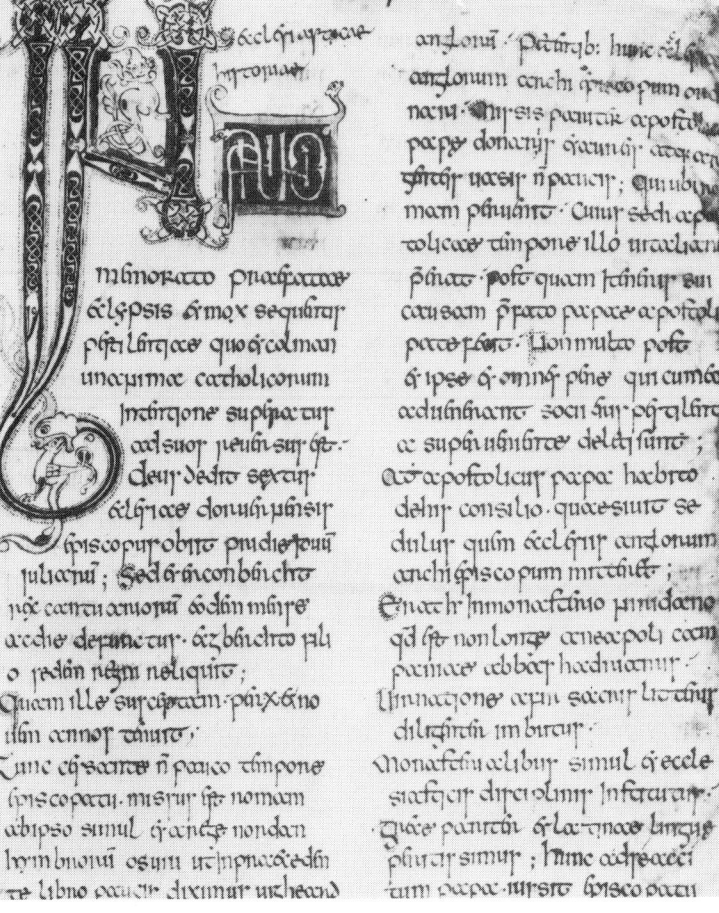

At the bottom of the opposite page is the picture of a page from the Lindisfarne Gospels – the beginning of St Matthew's Gospel. Some of the patterns are so small you can scarcely see them. Yet if you look at them under a magnifying glass you will notice how carefully they have been worked.

At one time in Anglo-Saxon England, the monasteries were full of beautiful books like these and of learned scholars and teachers. What had happened?

The coming of the Vikings

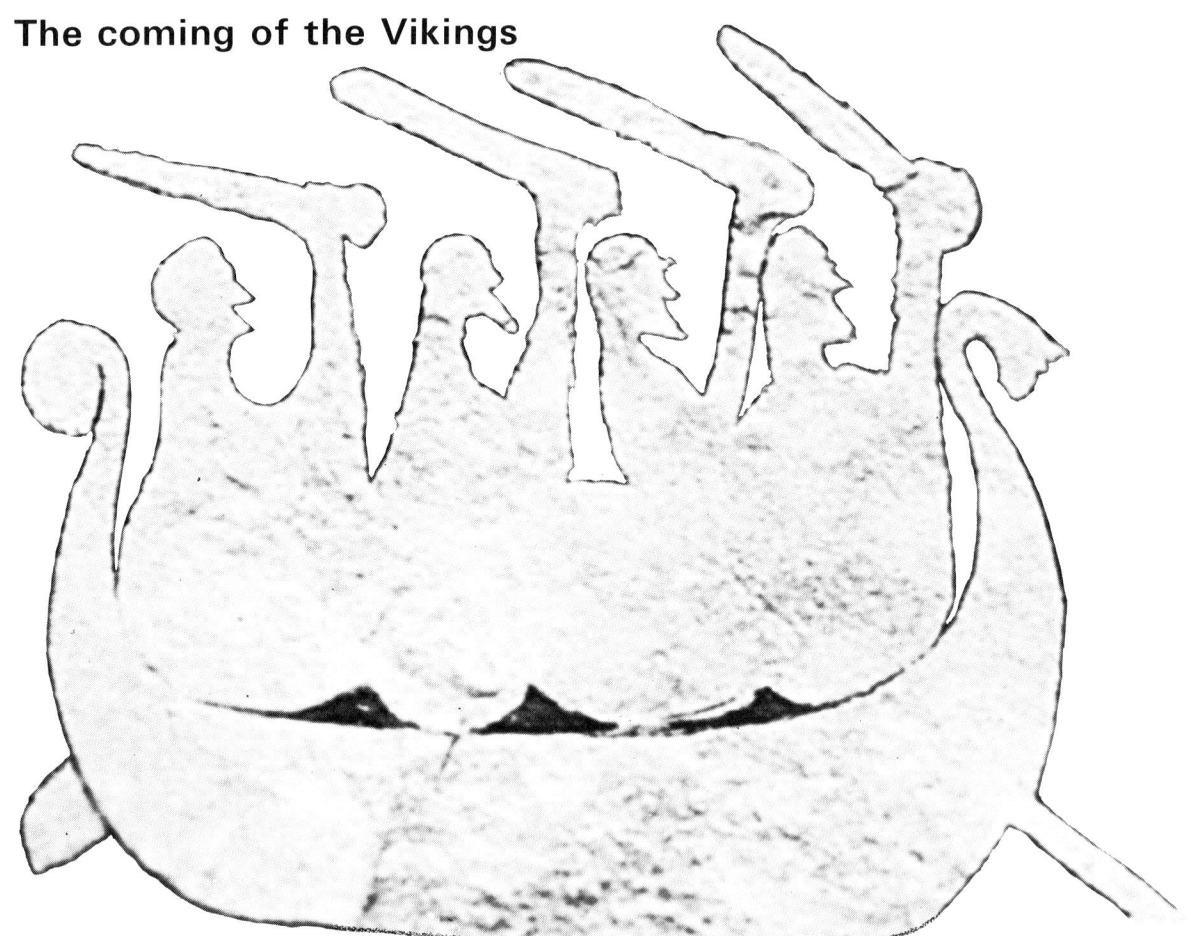

All this peaceful, civilised life had been brought to an end by the coming of the Vikings. They were warriors from Scandinavia, who came in raiding parties across the sea. Alfred himself said later, in one of his writings, that he had been told how the churches in England were full of books and treasures 'before it was all ravaged and burnt'.

The Anglo-Saxon Chronicle says about the year 793, 'the ravages of heathen men miserably destroyed God's church on Lindisfarne, with plunder and slaughter'.

These troubled times began before Alfred was born. He certainly would not have had very much time for learning to read and write, even if many of the monasteries where such things were taught had not been destroyed.

Who were these fierce Vikings?

They were brave, strong men who came from across the North Sea, from the countries we now call Norway, Sweden and Denmark. *The Anglo-Saxon Chronicle* usually calls them the 'Danes' wherever they came from — perhaps because the great armies that attacked the middle part of England were mostly Danish.

They came in their ships across the sea to the places
where they could most easily land, so that they raided
first the towns and villages, and particularly the rich
monasteries, on the east coast. Later they raided along
the Channel coast (on the continent of Europe as well
as in England) and up the big rivers.

Look carefully at the map.
Can you find the area
where you live? Would it
have been raided from the
sea by Vikings?

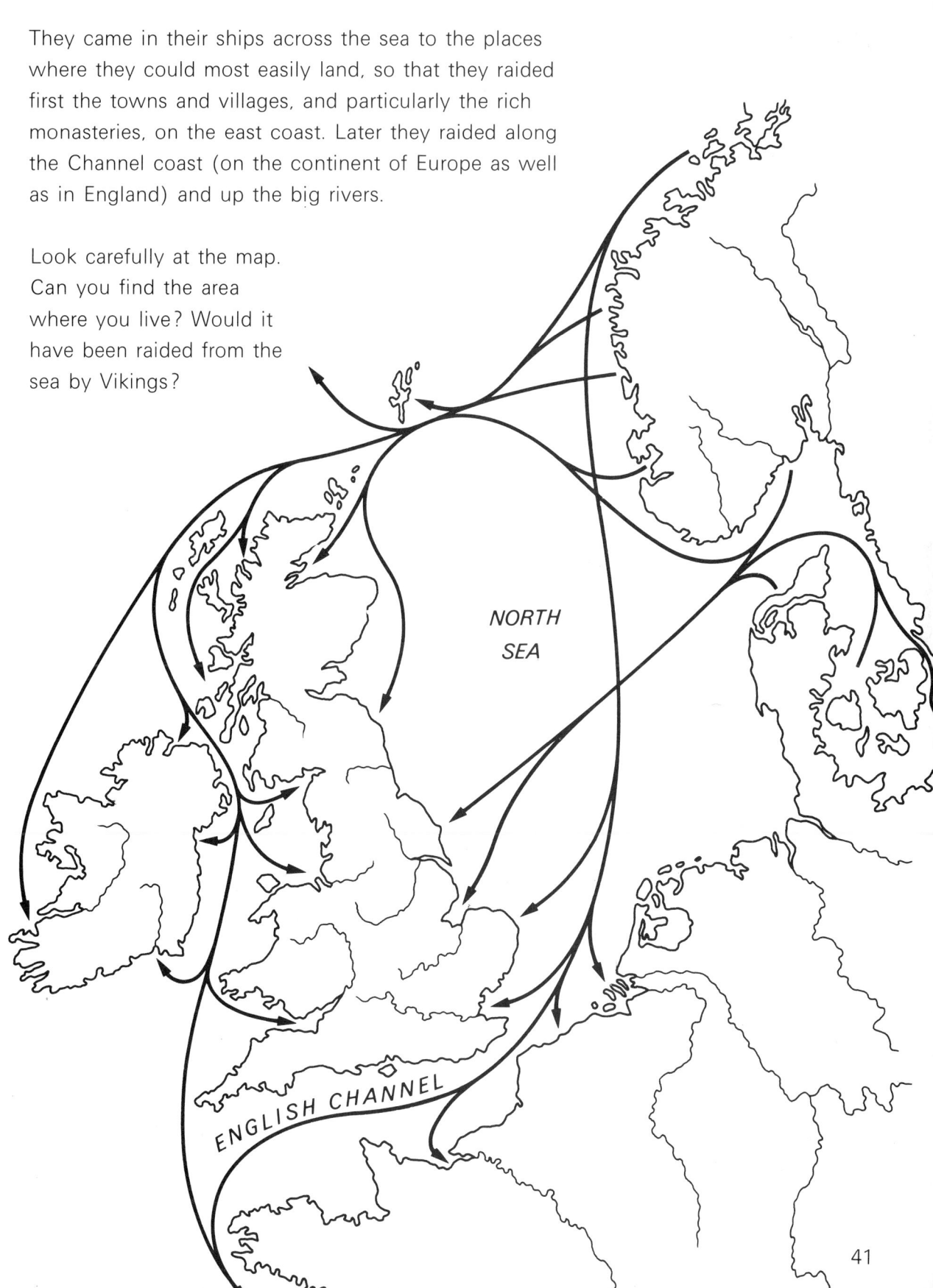

NORTH
SEA

ENGLISH CHANNEL

These Vikings came from lands where life was very hard and where the countryside would not grow enough food to keep all of them and their families alive. They were great fishermen and seafarers. They journeyed in their boats all over the world as it was known to them, trading and looking for new lands.

Here is one of their ships. It was found at Gokstad in Norway, with a chieftain and many of his goods buried inside it. It had a mast for sails and could also be rowed by 16 pairs of oars. Look for the oar-holes. The ship was only 23.33 metres long at its longest point. And yet men sailed these small wooden ships, not only across the North Sea, but also right across the Atlantic.

Find out the length of your classroom. How many times would it fit into this Viking ship? Find out the length of the *Queen Elizabeth II*. How many times would the Viking ship fit into the modern liner?

Below is a picture of a Viking ship on a Viking coin found at Birka in Sweden. It is a warship, as you can tell from the rowers' shields. How many rowers do you think there were on that side of the ship?

Here is a carving in bone of a Viking who might have rowed in that ship. This too, was found in Sweden.

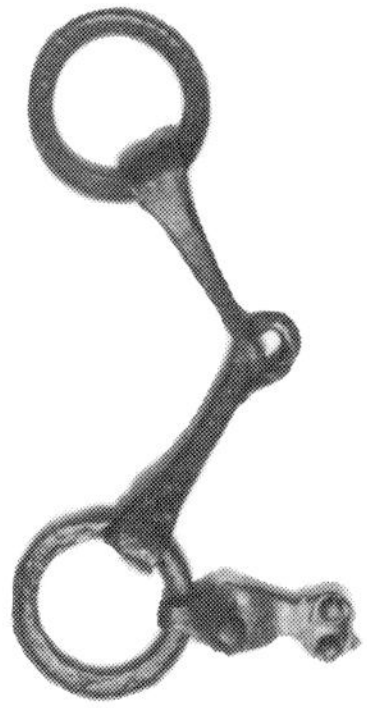

grave goods from
Asla

The Vikings believed in the Scandinavian gods, Odin and
Thor and many others. They thought that the gods were
warriors themselves and that it was good to die fighting.
They thought that it was right for the strongest fighter
to seize what he wanted and to keep it by force.

When a man died his most precious possessions, usually his weapons,
were often buried with him. Those shown above were found in the
grave of a man at Asla in Norway. He owned a huge sword (he
would probably have needed two hands for it), an axe, a spear, two
knives, a smaller axe or chopper, and a horse's bridle and a sickle as
well. Can you see which
is which? There is no
shield. Can you think
why that might be?

He might have worn a
helmet. Here is a
helmet from another
grave. It is strengthened
by two thick strips of
metal, crossing on top.
This would protect the
man's head if he was
attacked by a sword or
an axe.

Alfred's wars with the Vikings

But the Vikings were not just raiders, sailing out from Scandinavia in the good summer weather and sailing back before winter with the plunder they had seized. They were looking for new land in which to settle. To start with they came to the coastlands. *The Anglo-Saxon Chronicle* tells us that they first stayed over the winter at Sheppey, in Kent, in the year that Alfred's father died. Then they spread further into the country, fighting their way all the time because the Anglo-Saxons wanted to keep their own lands and possessions.

Viking graves and other things have been found in places far inland, showing just how far they reached and where the fighting took place.

This is an Anglo-Saxon sword hilt that was found in a Viking grave at Whitham in Yorkshire. Probably the Viking had won it from an Anglo-Saxon warrior.

This Viking sword and these other Viking objects were found in graves at Sonning Eye in Oxfordshire. Look carefully at the grave goods. You will easily spot the knife and the pin, but can you see that the others are arrowheads?

We know that there was much fighting in London. These are Viking spearheads, a Viking battleaxe and an Anglo-Saxon knife, all found in or near the Thames.

These nails were found at Walthamstow in Essex. They are rivets or clinch-nails from a Viking ship or boat. They were left after the wood had rotted away. A Viking was buried in it by the River Lea, along with his sword and spear and some ornaments. Probably he and his crew had sailed up the Lea from the Thames.

The Anglo-Saxon Chronicle also tells us some of the places the Vikings reached and where the Anglo-Saxons fought them — in Northumberland, Cheshire, Lincolnshire, East Anglia, Kent, Sussex, Hampshire, Dorset, Devon, Somerset. It was at Athelney in Somerset that Alfred is supposed to have burned the poor cottager's cakes. He was certainly in hiding there at the time.

Alfred and his men fought the 'Danes' over several years. Sometimes one side won, sometimes the other. But at last King Alfred and the Anglo-Saxons beat King Guthrum and his Danes at a great battle at Edington in Wiltshire. King Guthrum agreed to make peace, and he and his chief men were baptised Christians, at Aller in Somerset.

Find all the places mentioned on this page and the last one on a map. How near is the nearest to your home?

Find out more about:
— Viking ships — make drawings and notes
— Viking gods
— Viking weapons — show them on a chart.

45

This is an Anglo-Saxon font used to hold the water for baptisms or 'christenings'. It is from the church at Deerhurst, in Gloucestershire, but the one at Aller, where King Guthrum was baptised, must have looked very much like this. Look carefully at the patterns. Can you see how the spirals all join up with each other? This was a favourite pattern in Anglo-Saxon times and we can see it on many things — jewellery, metalwork and manuscripts. Probably it was woven into cloth too, so that people would wear it on their clothes.

King Alfred was King Guthrum's godfather at his baptism and the *Chronicle* says that he gave Guthrum and his companions many christening presents. Below is a picture of the sort of present Anglo-Saxons would give at a christening.

These spoons were found in the great ship-burial at Sutton Hoo, in Suffolk. It is almost certain that they were given to mark a baptism. Can you see the crosses on them?

Write a story in your book about being with King Alfred in his army at the time of the battle with King Guthrum and then the christening. Draw a picture showing Alfred giving gifts.

Alfred makes peace

Later, Alfred and Guthrum made a lasting peace. We still have copies of the document they drew up. It makes arrangements about such things as the fines that had to be paid to a man's relations if he were killed and the way in which the Anglo-Saxons and Danes could trade. Most important, it sets out the boundaries between the two sides. In it, Guthrum's men are called 'the people which is in East Anglia', so that must have been where they agreed to settle.

The peace treaty names the boundary as 'up the Thames, and then up the Lea to its source, then in a straight line to Bedford, then up the Ouse to Watling Street'. Notice how rivers and a Roman road are used as boundary marks, because they were unlikely to move or disappear.

Look carefully at the map and then see which side of the boundary line your home is. Use an atlas if you are not quite sure. Would you have been ruled by Alfred or by Guthrum?

That boundary was to last as long as England was divided between English and Vikings. The Viking side was to be called 'the Danelaw' because in it the laws and customs were different. But although the boundary lasted, the peace did not. Guthrum kept it as long as he lived, but after he died fighting broke out again.

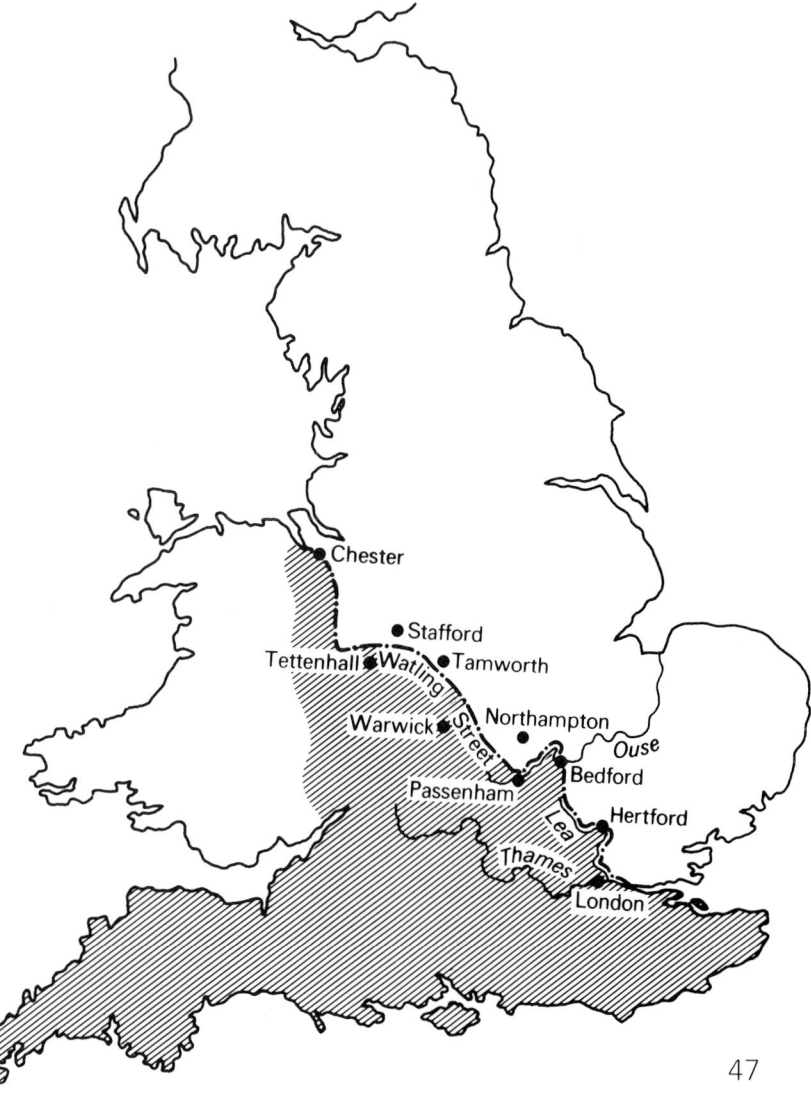

47

Alfred uses his peace

Anglo-Saxon
soldiers riding to
battle

When he had a short time of peace, Alfred had to organise his army so that it would be better prepared to fight if Wessex were attacked again. All Anglo-Saxon men had to be ready to fight. Each district had to send an armed man to serve the king for two months — but when the two months were up all the army went home! And if it was harvest time everyone went home to help anyway.

So the king arranged that his army should be in two halves — half to be out on service and the other half to be at home working the land. Then the two halves could change over at a given time.

All the richer men, who held land, had to make sure that their men came to serve in the army when the king wanted them. These rich men, or 'thegns' (pronounced 'thanes'), also had to serve. The king expected them to provide their own weapons as well as their men's. But no one had to provide uniforms. Everyone wore his own clothes and helmet, and a shirt of mail if he had one.

Alfred asked the landowners also to provide horses and to ride them when they served in the army. They did not fight from horseback, like cavalry, but they used horses to move quickly from place to place, instead of marching, which of course was slower. King Alfred learned this from his enemies. Their speed was one of the reasons why they had won so often.

48

Another thing that Alfred did while there was peace, was to build great walls round the larger towns and to fortify other places which could easily be defended. These fortified places were called 'burhs' in Anglo-Saxon and it is from them that many of our modern towns or 'boroughs' have developed.

Here are the present-day remains of one of the walls of a burh at Wareham, in Dorset. These are very high and steep even today. When the walls were built they would have been even steeper and there would have been no grass on them. It would have been very difficult for enemies to storm the high, slippery banks which would have been well defended by Alfred's army.

Below is an aerial photograph of another fortified place as it is today, Shaftesbury in Dorset. Shaftesbury is on the top of a very high steep hill which juts out, almost like an island, though today houses have been built up the slopes. All that Alfred had to do was build his wall across the narrowest point. Then he had a safe, strong fort inside the line marked on the photograph.

The Anglo-Saxon Chronicle tells us that another way in which Alfred prepared his people to fight the Danes was by building longships. Some people call this the beginning of the British navy. We don't quite know what Alfred's ships were like, but the *Chronicle* says that they were twice as long as the Viking ones and that some had 60 oars and some more. Look back at page 42. How many pairs of oars has that ship?

So Alfred's ships were faster than the Viking ones and also steadier. There were some fierce fights round the coasts. Sometimes Alfred's ships were able to chase the Vikings away from a harbour where they had planned to land.

This boat, which was found in the marshes at Graveney in Kent, may very well have been built in Alfred's day or perhaps a little later. It is not a warship, but a trading vessel, and is probably shorter than Alfred's longships. But if you look carefully you will see how sturdy it is, built for strength in rough seas. Notice how the planks overlap and how the stout cross-pieces of timber help to keep them in place.

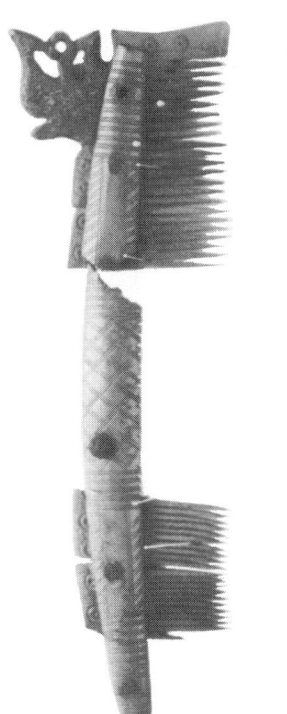

Though fighting against the Vikings was to go on for a very long time—until 1066 in fact—there was also quite often peace. Danes and Anglo-Saxons learned in some places to live side by side. In London, which King Alfred recaptured before his peace treaty with Guthrum, we find all sorts of remains which perhaps show that Viking families were living peacefully there, or that trading was taking place between the Anglo-Saxons and the Vikings.

These objects, for instance, all have Viking patterns on them. One is the remains of a comb, one is a piece of pottery (Roman pottery, in fact) and one is a piece of carved bone.

This collection of metal bits and pieces probably belonged to a Viking metal worker peacefully carrying on his trade in Lancashire. They are not pieces of weapons or armour, but broken bits of jewellery and ornament—probably the smith was going to make them into more bracelets or rings, or such like.

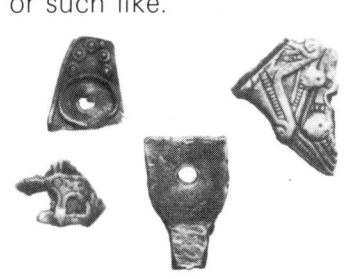

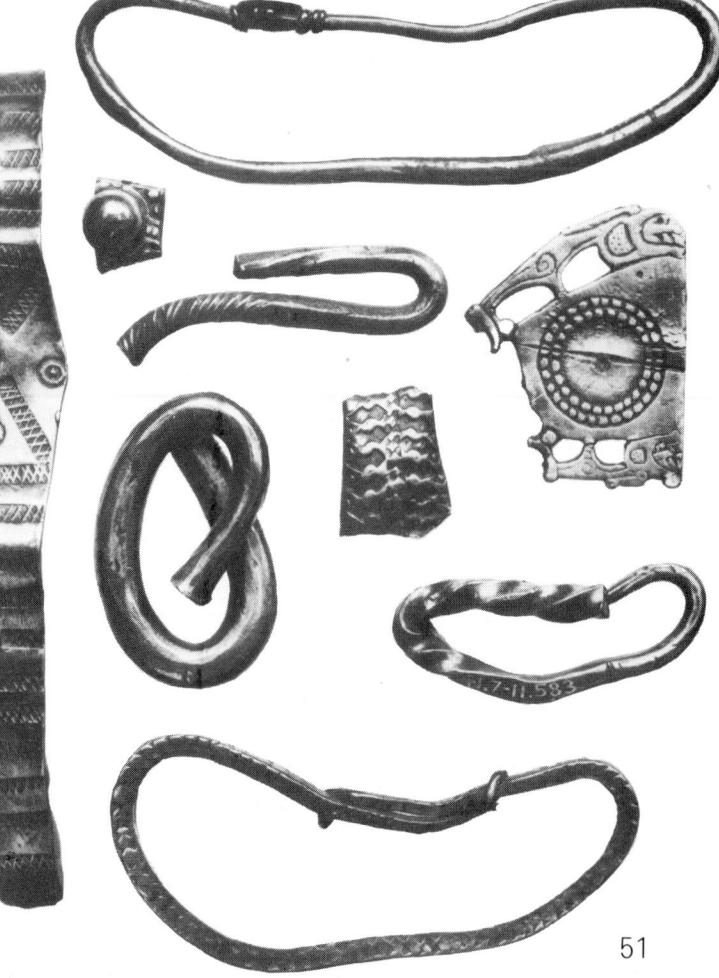

Alfred and the laws

When he had peace, King Alfred was very busy making things go better in his war-ravaged kingdom. One of the first things he did was to set the laws in order. He collected together all the laws of those who had been kings in England before him. He discussed them with his council and then kept those which he liked and left out the others. Then he added some laws of his own.

All these laws were very just and fair. Quite a lot were about the fines which had to be paid to the people who had been wronged. There is even a fine of 20 shillings for cutting off a man's beard. There are also laws about owning property. And there is one about the number of holidays in the year: 12 days at Christmas, 14 days at Easter, a week after harvest time and 4 separate days at various other times through the year.

This is a picture of an Anglo-Saxon king discussing laws with his council. Notice that it is not the king who is speaking. He is listening to what his councillors have to say.

Alfred and learning

Alfred was also very interested in schools and learning — perhaps because he himself learned to read so late. He set up a school at his court to teach reading and writing in both Latin and Old English. His own children were taught there and also, Bishop Asser says, in his book, *The Life of Alfred*, 'almost all the children of noble birth of the whole country'.

Alfred also helped the monasteries to start up their schools again and brought in learned men from Europe to show the monks what to do.

Do you remember that Aelfric's book was written for one of these monastery schools? (Look back to page 17.) There is one part of this book which describes the day of a boy at school. It is not very much like a present-day school.

The boys slept in the dormitory and were woken up by a bell while it was still dark. They had to go to church for all the services of the day. Most of these services were before midday, when the boys ate. They did not have lessons until the afternoon. Then they were very anxious to learn because they would be beaten if they did not! The only lessons they had were in reading and writing English and Latin.

School food was quite simple, but sounds good. 'I still eat meat, because I am a child,' says Aelfric's boy — some monks did not. There were also 'vegetables, eggs, fish, cheese, butter, beans and all clean things'. To drink he had 'ale, if I can get it, and otherwise water'.

This is a kind of bowl which Aelfric's schoolboys might very well have used for either eating or drinking. Do you see bowls shaped like this nowadays? What might you use them for?

Because King Alfred wanted as many people as possible to learn to read and to know things, he was anxious that there should be as many useful books in English as possible. He himself, among all the other tasks of his busy life, became a translator of Latin books into English. He wrote a very interesting Introduction to a translation of his, in which he tells us why he is a translator. 'It seems best to me,' he writes, 'to translate some of those books which are most necessary for all men to know, into the language we can all understand.'

Here is a piece of the manuscript of this Introduction. Alfred is writing about translation. The crossings-out and writings-in were done by someone later — just as we might scribble remarks in a book.

Some of the books which Alfred translated were about how priests and bishops ought to look after their people, about history and geography and about religion and philosophy.

He seems to have been very interested in history, because he also had translated Bede's *Ecclesiastical History* (see page 39), so that people could learn about their own country. He probably also arranged for the great *Anglo-Saxon Chronicle* to be written.

Because Alfred was always interested in learning new things, many travellers from other lands came to see him and tell him about their journeys. Some of these journeys were interesting enough for Alfred to put them into one of his books. There was a man called Ohthere, who travelled right round the north of Scandinavia, where no one had ever sailed before, and also down to the south. He described the voyage to Alfred, who put it in his book *Orosius*.

The map above shows where Ohthere went. Alfred also wrote about the voyage of Wulfstan who journeyed through the Baltic as far as the river Vistula, which is now in Russia. So King Alfred helped people to know more about the world and how big it was.

Alfred also received ambassadors from other lands and sent ambassadors out himself. These men did official business, such as paying church taxes, in such places as Rome and even as far away as Jerusalem. This Anglo-Saxon manuscript picture shows Jerusalem as Alfred's ambassadors may have seen it.

Building new minsters

Another thing that Alfred did with his peace was to build new minsters where the old ones had been destroyed by the Vikings and to enlarge old ones that he did not think were good enough, or perhaps were beginning to crumble away. (Remember that parts of the old ones may have been built only of wattle and daub and would not have lasted very long. To remind yourself, look back at the picture of North Elmham on page 33).

Some of our most famous cathedrals were built or rebuilt in the time of Alfred, his sons and grandsons. We do not always know what the minster of Alfred's time looked like—most of them have been rebuilt several times since then. We can get some idea from a few buildings and also from what archaeologists have found.

Here is something that many people think was made to look like a great church. It belonged to Aethelwald, Bishop of East Anglia in Alfred's time, and it may be like one of his minsters—perhaps North Elmham itself. It is, in fact, his seal-die— the mould for the seals on his important documents.

Here is the impression it makes. The piece of wax is stamped with the design that showed it belonged to the bishop. Notice the cross.

Try making your own seal-die from a potato cut. You could put your initials on it to show that it is yours. Use it to stamp the cover of the book you are making on the Anglo-Saxons.

Some of these cathedrals of course took a very long time to build or rebuild. Winchester was one of them. We are practically certain that work on it began at the end of the reign of King Alfred. Yet it was not finished until King Edgar's time—Edgar reigned from 959 to 975, so the cathedral took perhaps 60 or 70 years to build.

This beautiful picture shows King Edgar giving the charter of the finished minster to God—notice the charter in his hand. (A charter was a document about the ownership of land or buildings.)

If you look carefully at the bottom of this picture you will see how various kinds of people dressed. You have seen people dressed very like the lady on the left, on page 13. Notice the differences in clothes between the king and the monk on the right. Notice, too, the 'bald patch' on top of the monk's head. This is called a tonsure. The hair was shaved off in a circle. All monks had this as a sign that they were monks. (Look back at the picture on page 34 of the monks writing and copying books. You can just see their tonsures.)

Making new treasures

Another thing that Bishop Asser says that King Alfred did in time of peace, was to encourage goldsmiths and other craftsmen. Many beautiful things had, of course, been destroyed or carried off in the Viking raids and wars. Alfred was probably anxious that his land should have treasures again.

Here is a very beautiful object that has always been called the 'Alfred jewel' ever since it was found at Newton Park, in Somerset, quite near to Athelney where Alfred is known to have hidden during his time with the Danes. You saw a picture of the jewel on page 3 of this book. Now let us look at it more closely.

The portrait of a man in the centre may be a king, or may be a saint. The jewel is made of various coloured enamels. The man is wearing a green robe, the wand or sceptres are gold, the dividing lines are gold also and the sky is blue. All this picture is covered over with crystal, like glass over a painting. The surround is made of finely worked gold.

Here is the back of the Alfred jewel. It is made entirely of gold, with a leaf-like pattern engraved into it. Can you see how the front is joined on to the back, with little teeth turned over round the edge? You can also see, from this view of the jewel, that it looks as if it had been broken off something, perhaps a rod or long stick. No one knows what it can have been.

We do know, however, who had it made. There is lettering all round the jewel. It says, in Old English, 'AELFRED MEC HEHT GEWYRCAN' — in modern English 'ALFRED ORDERED ME TO BE MADE'.

There are other pieces of jewellery very like the Alfred jewel. Perhaps Alfred's craftsmen made them too. The one on the right is the Minster Lovell jewel, found at Minster Lovell in Oxfordshire. (You can see both it and the Alfred jewel in the Ashmolean Museum in Oxford.)

Though the centre-piece is not a picture but a pattern, it too is made of brightly coloured enamels and gold. The decoration round the edge is gold also. It is made with thin gold wire. This jewel, like the Alfred jewel, looks as if it belonged on the end of something – it even has a hole where it should be fastened on.

Another jewel very like these two is the Dowgate Hill brooch, found in London. The portrait in the centre is made of enamel and gold too, and the surround is of gold again, with little beads (called 'granulations'). But this time we do know that the jewel is a brooch, for there was a fastening on the back.

Draw pictures in your book of 'Jewels of King Alfred's day'. Colour them brightly with crayons or paints.

Making new towns

You will remember that, during the peace in the middle of his wars, Alfred ordered many fortified places, called burhs, to be built (see page 49). Sometimes these were walls built round towns that already existed, but sometimes they were new fortresses, built to be places of safety for the countryfolk around.

People came to live behind these walls, sometimes alongside people who were already living there. They helped to defend the walls. We can tell from the remains of bone, metal and pottery objects in these places that they did not all go away to their homes when peace came, but settled down to a town life. Trades sprang up—bone and metal working, pottery and weaving, as in Thetford. In Southampton, for instance, there were gravel roads. Foreign coins have been found, showing that there was trade with Europe.

Inside the burh walls it seems that the streets of these new towns were often laid out in a planned way—rather like a Roman town, in fact. Do you remember the walls of Wareham? (See page 49.) Inside those walls, many of the streets of today are still laid out as in Alfred's day. You can see this on the plan shown here.

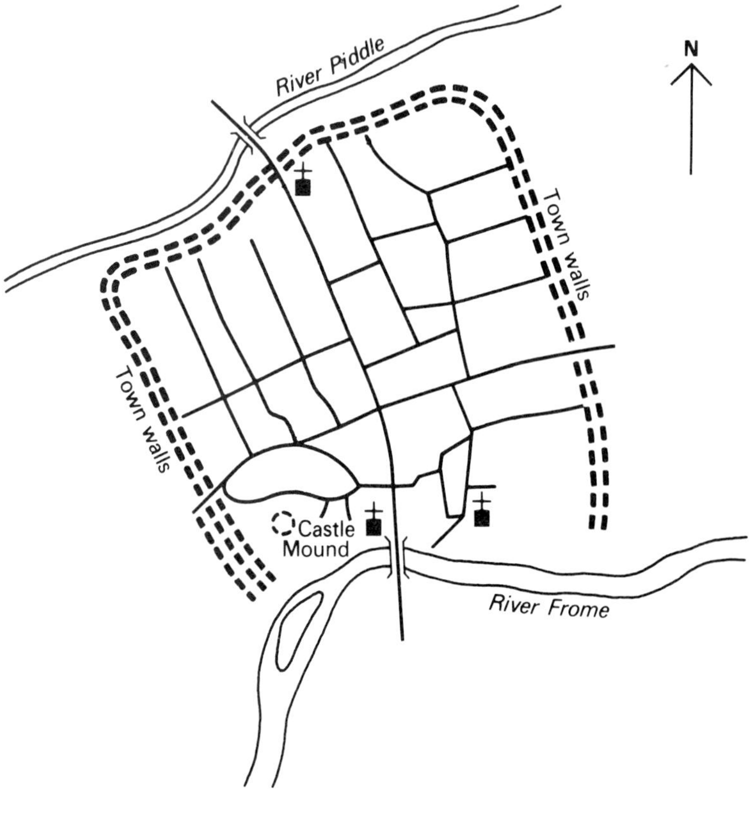

plan of Wareham

The townspeople built houses and prospered. Some of their household goods have been found and are in museums for us to see.

Winchester became very important and was the capital of Wessex and later of all England. It was probably at this time another of the planned towns. It had a new minster that was almost certainly started in Alfred's days.

On the right is a very handsome spouted pitcher from Winchester.

When some of these towns had become prosperous and important enough, they were allowed to have mints, where coins were struck, or made. Coins were not then made all in one place, as they are now, because it would have been difficult to move the money all over the country.

London, Winchester, Southampton, Oxford, Canterbury, Exeter and Gloucester were among the towns that had mints.

Here is a silver penny from London. It has Alfred's head on the 'head' side and the name of the mint town on the 'tail'. Can you make out the letters in the name for London (here spelt Londin)?

Here is a more difficult coin to read. Some people read this as Croydon. What do you think it might be?

Make up your own 'puzzle' mint-mark from the name of the place where you live.

Death of Alfred

Then in 900, after all his work, King Alfred died. He was 51 years old. We do not know where he died, although he was buried in Winchester. All that the *Chronicle* says of him at his death is:

'In this year Alfred the son of Aethelwulf departed, 6 days before All Saints' Day. [That is, on 26th October.] He was king over all the English people except that part which was under the Danes, and he had held the kingdom for 28½ years.'

But Alfred is remembered to this day. For very many years people told stories and sang songs about him as a brave man, and a wise and just king who did his best for his people and wanted peace for them. Hundreds of years later people called him 'the Great'.

His peace did not last. There were wars with the Vikings for the next 150 years or so, on and off. But some of his other work did last. His laws were kept by the English for a long time, his minsters were finished and became centres for worship and learning, his towns flourished, his schools went on. Most important perhaps, people continued to read and write and learn in English, their own language. Even after the Norman Conquest (1066) books were still written in English, including the *Chronicle* which Alfred had started. It may even be because of King Alfred that this book is written in English and not in Latin or French.

Write notes about:
- the schools which Alfred started
- the books he wrote
- the Alfred jewel
- the Minster Lovell jewel
- mints and coins.

Now that you have come to the end of this book, you may like to visit a museum where you will find some of the things that you have learned about. The museum in your local town may have objects from Anglo-Saxon times and even from King Alfred's day. There are such objects in the museums in London (the British Museum, the Guildhall Museum, the London Museum, the National Maritime Museum in Greenwich), Bristol, Cambridge (the Museum of Archaeology and Ethnology), Ipswich, Lewes, Lindisfarne, Liverpool, Norwich (the Castle Museum), Oxford (the Ashmolean Museum), Reading, Shaftesbury, Sheffield, Southampton (God's House Tower Museum), Thetford and Winchester (the City Museum). This map shows you where these places are.

When you visit a museum, make drawings and notes of things you see there and start your own Museum Book.

Index